What's Cooking on the PCT 2015

What's Cooking on the PCT 2015

Sponsored and Prepared by
Martin "Rainman" Leghart Jr.

Pacific Crest National Scenic Trail (PCT) Hikers, Angels, Friends, Family and Other Supporters and Followers contributed greatly to this book.

First Edition: November 2015

Printed in the United States of America

Available from Amazon.com, CreateSpace.com and other retail outlets.

ISBN: 978-1519377388

PACIFIC CREST TRAIL

ASSOCIATION

50% of all net profits from the sale of this book go to support the mission of the Pacific Crest Trail Association, to help protect, preserve and promote the Pacific Crest National Scenic Trail. Join the PCTA at www.PCTA.org

I dedicate this book to all the family, friends, trail angels and other supporters who made my trek possible, who fed me, drove me, housed me or otherwise encouraged me. Their acts, words and other magic brought me joy and happiness and otherwise made life more pleasant.

I want to give special recognition to my brother Jonathan and his wife Lonna (and maybe Alex) for managing my resupply boxes, gear changes, money, car and other personal effects while I was out taking a long walk. It would have been significantly more challenging without your love & support.

I'm happy and eager to share this book with my friends, wait...my family...from Branch Whitney's 52 Peak Club in Las Vegas, Nevada. I will be back to finish my deck Dinorah, I promise! Check out all the cool hikes they do at www.52peakclub.com. It's the most fun I've ever had in my life!

Here is a partial list of the 2015 hiker trash I met who made the journey more enjoyable:

Banjo	*Narwhal*
Bat	*Pop Top*
Bugs	*Possum*
Burgundy	*The Ravens*
Cookie Monster	*Snow White*
Dundee	*Speedy Gonzales*
Foxtrot	*Suds*
Hedgehog	*Sundown*
Juniper	*Treeman*
Karaoke	*Wall Street*
Morning Star	*Zig Zag*

Mile 563.1 – Cameron Canyon, near Mojave, California

Table of Contents

Want to learn more about this book, the project and the people behind it?

Go to www.cookingonthepct.com for more information.

You can sign up for updates, send us messages, learn about future books...and more!

Want to send a message to Rainman? That's easy: rainman@cookingonthepct.com

What's Cooking on the PCT 2015

Martin "Rainman" Leghart Jr.

Mile 213.0 — Mesa Wind Farm near San Gorgonio Pass, California

Preface

At the beginning of 2015 I began planning a thru hike of the Pacific Crest National Scenic Trail (PCT). I was in the midst of buying new gear, selling all my other personal possessions and moving to southern California. I used that location as my base of operations before my departure date in April. I couldn't be bothered with (nor did I feel I had the time) to purchase a dehydrator, experiment with it and/or search for recipes.

My menu consisted of pre-packaged foods of the Kraft, Knorr and Nissin brands. And I should have bought shares in Mrs. Debbie's and Kellogg's brands before my purchases, because I emptied entire shelves of those tasty pastries. For meats, I went with the standard foil pouches of tuna, salmon and Spam brand meat. I had to search a little harder for chicken and summer sausages in, more or less, single-serving quantities.

It wasn't until I got on trail and began meeting and talking and camping with the other hiker trash that I realized I was missing out on quite a bit. Gourmet foods, fantastically exquisite delights and some simple, yet delectable surprises were all around me. I seemed to be the only schmuck eating synthesized, processed foods. But by this time, my resupply boxes were already packed and waiting to ship.

I got the idea for putting together this book when I heard about a recipe involving Top Ramen brand instant noodles and peanut butter. It sounded interesting. And then I heard about ramen instant noodles and Idahoan brand instant mashed potatoes. Well wait a minute! Now we're talking about the same types of foods I'm carrying. Tell me more!

And there's more to tell...

Acknowledgements

This book would not be possible without the generosity of all the recipe contributors. These wonderful hikers, angels, friends, family, supporters and followers of the PCT came together as a community and donated their time and effort – and their recipes – for the betterment of this publication. Their tasty and unusual concoctions are an integral part of this book. Thank you for your contributions.

It is also important to recognize the men and women of the Pacific Crest Trail Association. It is because of their (and their volunteers') diligence, efforts, hard work and dedication to the PCT that so many can experience such an amazing journey. With regard to this book, we especially acknowledge PCTA's patience, understanding and belief in this project before we even got to the launching pad. Thank you so very much!

Mile 277.0 – Bertha Ridge just north of Big Bear City, California

Introduction

Every hiker knows food is energy. But food is also weight. Oh, but food also brings a sense of comfort and ease to an otherwise tired body and bleary mind. And if there are tasty treats your loved one stashed in your resupply box – those could be your biggest delights!

I feel that choosing the right foods for your long distance hike – or any outing where you'll be away from civilization for an extended period of time – is more art than science.

When I was preparing for my PCT journey I was looking at food supply in a very scientific fashion. I researched high and low to find out how many calories I would burn on any given day. Estimating that I would be hiking 21.33 miles, with 2,485 feet of elevation gain on average per day, I somehow surmised I would burn about 3,750 calories each day. The problem was, I was only able to pack and consume 3,000 calories per day. This meant I was in a caloric deficit of about 750 calories per day.

And my food didn't taste very good. I went with pre-packaged meals (Kraft brand Macaroni & Cheese, Knorr brand Pasta & Rice Side Dishes, Mountain House brand, Nissin Top Ramen brand instant noodles, Idahoan brand potatoes, etc.). I would couple those with Old Wisconsin brand summer sausage, Hormel brand Spam, Tyson brand chicken, tuna or salmon to bring up the protein value. Overall, though, it wasn't very exciting.

It's no wonder that when I'd roll into town it wasn't at all uncommon for me to consume 10,000 calories of restaurant and/or fast food in a single day. After 5 or 6 or 7 days of hiking, my body (according to the above calculation) is in deficit 4,000 or 5,000 calories (aka "hiker hunger"). I'm also craving new tastes, and my metabolism is still in overdrive, even on zero days.

I remember getting to Cajon Pass around 9:30am and meeting up at McDonald's with all the usual suspects. I ordered a deluxe breakfast meal, orange juice and cinnamon roll bites – conservatively, 2,200 calories. And that was second breakfast (I ate before I broke camp earlier that morning).

At 10:30am, when they began serving lunch, I (on a bet from some of the other hiker trash) ordered the McGangbang – a secret menu item consisting of a McChicken patty inside of a Double Quarter Pounder with cheese. To make it a meal, I ordered french fries, a chocolate shake and a Diet Coke. That was elevenses.

At around 1:00pm, Dundee and I headed across the highway to the Best Western so he could pick up his resupply box. I waited for him at Del Taco. After he returned, we ate a few tacos, probably a burrito and some french fries. We headed out later that afternoon, logged about 5 miles and found a dry wash just off the trail in Swarthout Canyon before the

1

road. We fixed supper and dined with Pop Top and Karaoke. That was a lot of food in one day. But we felt good.

One of the reasons I decided to put this book together is to allow the community to learn from one another about the foods they prepare and pack. At home I'm a half-way decent cook, but as I referenced earlier, I knew nothing about dehydrating foods, and I didn't want to take any chances so late in the game. My pre-packaged, processed meals weren't so great, I'll admit that. Will I do it differently next time out? Absolutely! Especially with all the tasty delights found in this book!

I will say one more thing. I discovered early on in the hike that even though we all stunk like you know what, we all seemed to have an over developed sense of smell. I remember hiking with Narwhal on the way to Big Bear when we both could "smell" the day hikers heading in the opposite direction. They just smelled so clean and fresh – an enveloping aroma of jasmine and sandalwood, as I recall.

Fast forward to just before Tehachapi, I was hiking with Juniper. We found a little dirt patch 10 to 15 yards off the trail to set up camp for the night. Earlier, she and I agreed that it would be Kraft brand macaroni and cheese night – a comforting and rewarding meal for the long and tiring day. We got our tents set up and sat our butts down on a log and began boiling our noodles. A minute later Sprout and her gang – still making steps along the trail – hesitated mid-stride, turned to us and said "Yum! Smells like mac-n-cheese."

Food, indeed, is a hiker's best friend. Hiker trash can smell food from long distances, and they can consume food faster (and in larger quantities) than most. On the following pages you'll find recipe contributions from fellow PCTers...a collection of meals, snacks, beverages and desserts that are calorically dense, easy to make, light to pack, and oh so tasty. Use this book to help prepare for your next great adventure. Buy copies for your friends, family and fellow hikers and outdoors adventurists. Above all else, make sure you're a part of next year's edition of What's Cooking on the PCT!

— Rainman

Vegan & Vegetarian Dishes

Mile 444.4 – Soledad Canyon near Acton, California

Barking Spider Bean Burritos

Bean Burrito with cheese and hot sauce.

Best for **Lunch | Dinner | Snack**

Servings: **3**

Requires At-Home Prep:	**No**	On-Trail Prep Time:	**2 minutes**
Prep Time:	**none**	Cook Time:	**2 minutes using hot water**
Cook Time:	**none**		

Extra beans can be eaten with Pringles brand tortilla chips. Pringles brand chips stay uncrushed in their can while hiking and make for a great trash can when empty.

1 cup dehydrated refried beans, Amazon.com

1 cup water (hot or cold)

1 tbsp olive oil

3 tortillas (corn or flour)

3 packets Taco Bell brand hot sauce

3 packets parmesan cheese (from a pizza place)

Instructions:

1. Mix 1 cup of dehydrated refried beans with 1 cup of water (hot or cold) together in a quart size Ziploc brand bag. If using cold water plan 1 hour for rehydration.

2. Add 1 tbsp of olive oil for extra fat and to keep the beans from sticking to the baggie.

3. Seal bag and knead with hands.

4. Using a spork, spoon beans onto tortillas. Top with hot sauce and parmesan cheese.

www.bjandclara.blogspot.com

"Country Mouse" and "Shadow" - Anytown, US

Thru Hiker | 2015

Image Credit: Country Mouse

Best Ever Vegan Chili Stew

Quick spicy chili, Discovered it at a family gathering on the Oregon Coast. Dehydrated it this year for a kayak trip in the San Juans. YUMM! Very good for feeding a crowd at home or freezing for later. You can add toppings – grated cheese, green onion, sour cream, etc.

Best for **Dinner**

Servings: **15 to 20**

Requires At-Home Prep:	**Yes**	On-Trail Prep Time:	**none**
Prep Time:	**20 minutes**	Cook Time:	**10 minutes**
Cook Time:	**25 minutes + dehydrating**		

Smash beans after cooking so they will dehydrate more quickly. Also, break tomatoes into smaller pieces - before cooking! Experiment with amount of water and time to "cook" for rehydrating. I like it best when it is thick, not soupy :O) Remember to recycle all the cans!

2 **cups** onion, chopped	2 **cans** black beans	2 **tsp** chili powder
2 **green peppers**, chopped	2 **cans** pinto beans	2 **tsp** ground cumin
2-4 **cloves** garlic, chopped fine	2 **cans** garbanzo beans	3/4 **tsp** salt
4 **cans** stewed tomatoes	3 **large cans** tomato sauce	
2 **cans** kidney beans	1-1/3 **cups** salsa	

Instructions:

1. Saute onions, green peppers and garlic.

2. Add stewed tomatoes, beans, tomato sauce, salsa, chili powder, cumin and salt.

3. Simmer for 20 minutes.

4. Spread pretty thin on plastic sheets that come with some dehydrators, or cookie sheets in the oven--lowest temp, door ajar. Time to dehydrate will vary.

5. Rehydrate and cook.

Kay S. - Boise, ID, US

Family-Friend | Supporter-Follower | 2007 to 2015

Breakfast Bomb!

A perfect breakfast drink for long distance hikes. Get your coffee fix, vitamins, minerals, protein, and calories all in one warming drink. I drank this every morning on my 2014 PCT Hike.

Best for **Breakfast**

Servings: **2**

Requires At-Home Prep:	**Maybe**	On-Trail Prep Time:	**2 minutes**
Prep Time:	**2 minutes**	Cook Time:	**2 minutes**
Cook Time:	**none**		

Mix the powders in advance and store in a snack sized Ziploc brand bag for each day to take on the trail.

2 packets Starbucks brand VIA coffee

1/2 packet Carnation brand Instant Breakfast, any flavor

2 tbsp Carnation brand Instant non-fat dry milk powder

16 oz water

Instructions:

1. Bring water to a boil and combine with dry ingredients in a Nalgene brand bottle.

2. Shake.

3. Share it with a friend or drink it all!

http://jandjnorthbound.wordpress.com

Jean "Lady Luck" T. - Seattle, WA, US

Section Hiker | 2014

Breakfast Shake

Just mix with water and drink. Tastes like a chocolate peanut butter milkshake and is great for breakfast or a quick burst of calories anytime during the day.

Best for **Breakfast | Snack | Beverage**

Servings: **1**   Calories: 780   Protein (g): 40

Requires At-Home Prep:	**Yes**	On-Trail Prep Time:	**2 minutes**
Prep Time:	**2 minutes**	Cook Time:	**none**
Cook Time:	**none**		

Bring a cleaned out peanut butter jar. Fill it with the powder and some water and shake. Can also be made in a pot, but the peanut butter jar is much easier, fairly light, essentially free, and can be an extra water bottle in a pinch.

3/4 cup Nido brand dehydrated whole milk

2 packets Nestle brand hot chocolate mix

1/3 cup Byrd Mill brand 28% fat peanut flour

cinnamon to taste (optional)

Instructions:

At Home Prep:

1. Mix all ingredients in a plastic baggie for storage.

Trail Prep:

2. Add mixture to a vessel with water and stir or shake.

Kyle "Sundance" W. - Harpswell, ME, US
Section Hiker | 2014

Peter Y.
Section Hiker | 2014

Tim "Mrs. Dash" H.
Section Hiker | 2014

Vegetarian

Couscous With Pinenuts

This packs a lot of calories for the weight and space. It reconstitutes well at high elevation. Staple on our section from Muir Trail Ranch through Forester Pass to Trail Pass where we needed every inch of space in the bear canister.

Best for **Dinner**

Servings: **1**   Calories: 760

Requires At-Home Prep:	**Maybe**
Prep Time:	**10 minutes**
Cook Time:	**none, unless dehydrating carrots**
On-Trail Prep Time:	**5 minutes to boil water**
Cook Time:	**10 minutes sitting in cozy**

1/2 box Near East brand Pinenut couscous

1/2 cup Kraft brand parmesan cheese, shelf stable

2 tsp chicken bouillon

1/4 cup Trader Joes brand Dry Roasted Pinenuts

1/4 cup dehydrated carrots

1/4 cup Nido brand dried milk

1-1/2 cups boiling water

1/4 cup dried mushrooms, from Asian section in grocery

Instructions:

Dehydrate carrots:

1. Peel and slice thinly fresh carrots.

2. Pour boiling over carrots to blanch and let sit 2-5 minutes then drain and blot dry.

3. Spread on dehydrator tray and dry 6 hours or place on cookie sheet and dry in low oven until dry.

To prepare:

4. Add all ingredients to freezer bag.

5. Pour boiling water into bag and let sit 10 minutes in cozy.

6. Alternate: add mix to 1-1/2 cups boiling water in pan and let sit.

Judy "Plan B" F. - Issaquah, WA, US

Section Hiker | 2005 to 2015

Vegetarian | Nut Free

Hete Bliksem - Hot Lightning

Idahoan brand is quick and filling. We tried several combi's of food. This looks like a real old dutch recipe called "hete bliksem," which translates to "hot lightning." Although it's not hot but really tasteful.

Best for **Dinner**

Servings: **2**   Calories: **880**

Requires At-Home Prep: **No**
Prep Time: **none**
Cook Time: **none**

On-Trail Prep Time: **1 minute**
Cook Time: **3 minutes**

Instead of the apples also try dried mango or apricots. Instead of four cheese you can try a different Idahoan brand flavor, as long as it has some cheese in it. The spice mix can also be a standard Moroccan spice mix.

2 packages Idahoan brand 4 Cheese mashed potatoes, 113-gram packages; cook according to instructions
150 grams dried apples, cut into smaller pieces
A few grams cinnamon - clove - pepper spice mix

Instructions:

1. Bring water to a boil. Add apples and let it boil for 1 minute.

2. Remove from heat. Add spice mix and let it stand for a few minutes until apples are soft and swollen.

3. Add mashed potatoes and serve directly.

Lian "Cookie Monster" D. - Horendonk, Antwerp, Belgium

Vegetarian | Vegan | Shellfish Free | Dairy Free | Nut Free | Egg Free | Sugar Free | Low Fat | Kosher | Halal | Words of Wisdom

Leebe – FRESH Baked Bedouin Bread

Light, cheap and great. Are you tired of eating the same old crumbling tortillas and cold week old bread on trail? I was, so after a few weeks on the PCT, whenever I was able to, I went back to the old Bedouin Leebe I learned to make while hiking in the Israeli desert. Be able to bake your own, on trail, hot, fresh flat bread-bread-cake-focaccia or anything else your imagination come up with.

Best for **Breakfast | Lunch | Dinner | Dessert | Snack | Appetizer | Side Dish**

Servings: **3**

Requires At-Home Prep:	**No**	
Prep Time:	**none**	
Cook Time:	**none**	

On-Trail Prep Time: **30 to 40 minutes**
Cook Time: **15 to 20 minutes**

1. This recipe is for fire making hikers, only possible where it is legal, safe and possible to make a campfire and takes some time.

Image Credit: Eric Yellin

2. This is a very simple and basic version of the Leebe. I encourage you to get creative and make any innovations you can think of. For example, adding sugar, coco powder, mile powder and honey to make a cake, fill the leebe with meat or cheese, or add yeast to the mix to let the bread rise.

3. You can also add a handful of sunflower seeds or nut mix.

1 arms-full small to medium pieces of wood

1 lb flour

1-2 cups water

1 splash olive oil

1 pinch salt

handful of sunflower seeds or nut mix (optional)

Instructions:

1 If legal and safe to do so, make a fire; turning the wood into coal.

2. While the fire is burning, pour the flour on a clean concave surface (Ex: rock; I like digging a shallow hole in the ground and placing a plastic bag on top); leave some flour on the side for later.

3. Pour the water onto the flour slowly while mixing the mixture until it turns in the a nice smooth dough. Refrain from pouring too much water or the dough will turn too sticky (and so will the situation).

4. Add olive oil and salt and keep kneading the dough for about 2 minutes or until it turns malleable. You can add sunflower seeds or any other nut mix.

5. Flatten the dough until it gets round and one inch thick.

6. Cover the dough with the flour you put aside.

7. Using a stick, dig a bed in the coals; put the loaf inside and cover it with the coals.

8. Let the dough bake for about 5-10 minutes until it becomes hard and darkens. You can poke a hole to see that the inside isn't still doughy. Flip it around and repeat the process; the outside may get burned, don't worry.

9. Take it out of the fire and beat the loaf up to break off the burnt crust and to shake off the dust.

10. DIG IN (:

Yuval "The Messenger" Y. - Sderot, Israel

Thru Hiker | 2013

Vegetarian

Marzipan Tortillas

Very easy, tasteful and full of energy to run up that mountain.

Best for **Lunch**

Servings: **4**   Calories: **1000**

Requires At-Home Prep: **No**

Prep Time: **none**

Cook Time: **none**

On-Trail Prep Time: **1 minute**

Cook Time: **none**

Instead of marzipan also an almond paste roll (baking section) can be used. This is more soft and less dry.

4 medium size white tortillas

1 roll marzipan, 200 grams

Instructions:

1. Cut marzipan roll in 20 thin slices.

2. Add 5 slices in one line in the middle of the tortilla.

3. Make a roll and enjoy the tortilla.

4. Prepare the other three tortillas as above.

5. Eat 2 tortillas each.

Lian "Cookie Monster" D. - Horendonk, Antwerp, Belgium

Thru Hiker | 2015

Vegetarian | Vegan | Dairy Free | Nut Free | Kosher

Miso Ramen a la Grouch

A nutritious take on traditional ramen with a spicy punch!

Best for **Lunch | Dinner | Snack**

Servings: **1**   Calories: **600**

Requires At-Home Prep: **Maybe**

Prep Time: **none**

Cook Time: **none**

On-Trail Prep Time: **3 minutes** to **1 hour**

Cook Time: **5 minutes**

Miso Ramen a la Grouch works hot or cold - with cold hydrating stoveless systems, coozie cooking or traditional canister stove preparation.

I usually go stoveless, so I'll include preparation instructions for that method. Of course, if you like hot food, simply boil the water first, add ingredients and enjoy in your vessel of choice! I would recommend against preparing hot food in your peanut butter jar, as the heat reshapes the plastic and the jar won't seal!

8 oz purified water

1 to 1-1/2 packages ramen noodles, type is unimportant; we discard the included flavor packet

1 envelope Edwards & Sons brand Miso-Cup Original Golden Vegetable Soup

1 tbsp Native Forest brand Coconut Milk Powder

1 dash Tapatio brand hot sauce or other hot sauce, to taste (or 1 convenience store hot sauce packet)

1 dash ground black pepper, to taste

1/2 oz packet soy sauce, to taste

1 pinch dehydrated seaweed. if available

1/4 cup trail sprouts, if available

Instructions:

1. In a clean peanut butter jar (or one with PB residue - the PB flavor adds a lil' something to the dish) crush ramen noodles into bits (crushed noodles are easier to spoon, and occupy less space). Add miso packet, coconut milk powder, hot sauce, pepper, soy sauce, seaweed, and delicious filtered spring water.

2. Place lid on PB jar. Shake the sh*t out of it.

3. Place in pack and walk 3 miles or 1 hour.

4. Noodles can be consumed after 20 minutes if you prefer al dente (or are freakin' starving) and will be fine up to 4 hours after rehydration.

5. If you're trail sprouting - using a hemp bag to germinate some alfalfa or clover sprouts or other hippy ish - they work great with this dish, adding a little zip and fresh flavor. Add the sprouts after the noodles are fully hydrated. I recommend the trail sprouting bag from Outdoor Herbivore and ordering organic sprouts from The Sprout House - tho pretty much any co-op along the PCT will have sprouting seeds available.

6. Get out that titanium spork and enjoy!

www.songsoutofthecity.com

GROUCHO Le MIEUX - Seattle, WA, US

Thru Hiker | 2015

Vegetarian

No Cook Vegetarian Couscous In Tortilla

It's a homemade just add water couscous, vegetable and nut mixture that tastes great on a flour tortilla or plain. Can be served as lunch or dinner. It's vegetarian, but not vegan. Can be real spicy if a whole package of crushed red peppers is used.

Best for **Lunch | Dinner**

Servings: **1**

Requires At-Home Prep:	No	On-Trail Prep Time:	15 minutes
Prep Time:	3 minutes	Cook Time:	none
Cook Time:	none		

Adding a little bit too much water to rehydrate the couscous is optional as it just means more parmesan cheese will be added after to thicken the mixture up. Makes it more cheesy.

1/2 cup couscous

4 tbsp Winco brand vegetable blend soup mix

3 tsp pine nuts

4 tsp almonds, shredded

1 tbsp instant refried beans

1 tsp onion flakes

1/2 tsp salt

1/2 tsp pepper

1 package Pizza Hut brand crushed red peppers

1-1/2 cups water

3-4 tbsp shelf-stable parmesan cheese

2 flour tortillas

Instructions:

1. Add all dry ingredients except the parmesan and flour tortillas to a rehydration jar or quart freezer Ziploc brand bag.

2. Add cold water to dry ingredients and stir. Let the mixture rehydrate for 10-15 minutes.

3. Add parmesan cheese and stir well. If too soupy, add an extra tablespoon of parmesan. If too thick add a little more water.

4. Add cayenne to your liking and serve wrapped up in a flour tortilla.

Julia "Cayman" S. - Georgetown, Cayman Islands

Thru Hiker | Section Hiker | 2015

Vegetarian

Oatmeal Hawaii

No more boring Quaker brand oatmeals which gives you hunger within half an hour. Make your own tropical oatmeal which lasts a few hours without a hungry feeling

Best for **Breakfast**

Servings: **1**

Requires At-Home Prep:	No	On-Trail Prep Time:	1 minute
Prep Time:	none	Cook Time:	6 minutes
Cook Time:	none		

Keep it warm while oatmeal is soaking.

50 grams plain oatmeal

25 grams coconut pieces

25 grams dried bananas

25 grams dried pineapple

25 grams whole pecan nuts

2 sticks sugar

10-20 grams dried milk powder

Instructions:

1. Premix oatmeal, coconut, bananas, pineapples and pecan nuts.

2. Add oatmeal mix into a big cup.

3. Add sugar and milk on top

4. Bring 1 cup of water to a boil.

5. Add boiled water into the cup. Oatmeal should be covered with at least 1 cm of hot water.

6. Stir and let it stand for 5 minutes in a warm place until oatmeal is soft.

Lian "Cookie Monster" D. - Horendonk, Antwerp, Belgium   Thru Hiker | 2015

Vegetarian | Dairy Free | Nut Free | Egg Free

Quick And Dirty Peach Cobbler

I first came across the Louisiana Fish Fry brand Cobbler mix while stocking up for a trip to Desolation Wilderness in California. I added a bag of dried peaches to my cart and thought "what could go wrong?" I decided to surprise my friends, and didn't tell them until after dinner that I had brought this along. After 45 minutes of staring at me salivating, we devoured this tasty treat (even the sides that had gotten crispy and burnt from over cooking)! It was immediately declared that this would have to be added to every future trip possible, and we haven't missed a beat yet! Hope you enjoy it as much as we did.

Best for **Dessert**

Servings: **3 to 5**

Requires At-Home Prep:	No	On-Trail Prep Time:	**5 minutes**
Prep Time:	none	Cook Time:	**35 to 45 minutes**
Cook Time:	none		

If your local super market does not carry this brand of cobbler mix, it can also be found online. As an added delicacy, you can combine the cut up peaches to the 1 cup of water as far ahead of time as you like.If you are using a traditional pot (not non-stick), add a little bit of oil to coat the sides.

10.58 oz package Louisiana Fish Fry brand Cobbler Mix

1 cup water, use just enough to create smooth consistency in batter

1-2 oz olive oil

8-10 pieces dried (not dehydrated) peaches, cut pieces in half (or quarters)

3 packets turbinado sugar, used to as glaze melted on top (optional)

Instructions:

1. Add cobbler mix to pot; stir in enough water and oil to create a smooth batter.

2. Cut and add dried peaches into batter.

3. Cook off to the side of small to medium fire rotating often! Where fires are prohibited, or a danger, cook using the round-the-clock method on a normal backpacking stove. If safe, add a twiggy fire on top of the lid for more even cooking.

4. If adding optional sugar glaze, do so approximately 5 minutes before you expect the cobbler to be done.

5. Cooks in 35-45 minutes; check doneness with a knife or spoon handle. Should pull out cleanly (or mostly clean if you prefer a more gooey affair).

6. Dig in with everyone who has been staring and salivating for the past 45 minutes!

Sam "Mac" A. - San Jose, CA, US

Section Hiker | 2012 to 2015

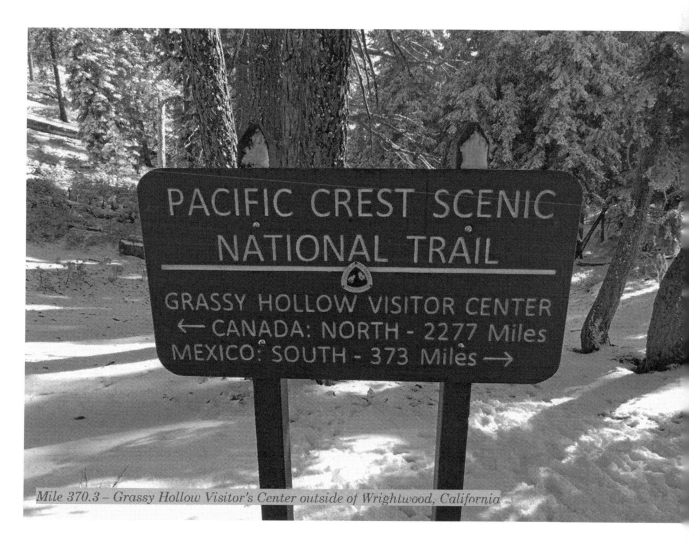

Mile 370.3 – Grassy Hollow Visitor's Center outside of Wrightwood, California

Ramen Pad Thai

Freezer bag style dinner in a bag using dry Pad Thai mix and coconut cream powder from the local Asian market.

Best for **Dinner**

Servings: **1**   Calories: **885**

Requires At-Home Prep: **Yes**   On-Trail Prep Time: **none**
          Prep Time: **10 minutes**   Cook Time: **15 minutes**
          Cook Time: **none**

This recipe goes on every trip!

1 package ramen noodles, crush; discard spices   **1/4 cup** dry roasted peanuts

1/2 package pad Thai peanut mix; Asian grocer   **2 tbsp** coconut cream powder

1/2 cup freeze dried peas

Instructions:

1. Place all ingredients in a Ziploc brand pint freezer bag.

2. Add boiling water to cover and let sit 15 minutes in a cozy or under your stocking hat.

Alternate: Can also be added directly to about 1-1/2 cups of boiling water in the pan.

Judy "Plan B" F. - Issaquah, WA, US   Section Hiker | 2005 to 2015

Vegetarian | Gluten Free | Nut Free | Egg Free | Sugar Free

Wicked Good Loaded Mashed Potato Bowl

Those pre-made "just add water" mashed potato packs from the store are decent. But let's be honest, they need way more awesome tasty goodies mixed in and they're too darn small for a hungry hiker!

Best for **Breakfast | Lunch | Dinner**

Servings: **1**

Requires At-Home Prep: **Yes**
          Prep Time: **5 minutes**
          Cook Time: **none**

On-Trail Prep Time: **none**
          Cook Time: **2 minutes sitting, plus time to boil water**

Mix at home, store in baggies, customize it the way you want it!

1 cup water

1-1/3 cups Idahoan brand Original instant mashed potato flakes

2 tbsp nutritional yeast

2 tbsp Kraft brand powdered parmesan cheese

1 tsp granulated garlic

1/4 tsp ground black pepper

1 cup Fritos brand corn chips, crushed

2 tbsp dried bacon pieces, if desired

2 tbsp dehydrated soup veggies (onion, parsley, carrot, celery), look for these in the bulk foods section of the grocery store

Instructions:

1. Boil 1 cup of water.

2. Dump everything else in a bowl.

3. Add boiling water, stir well.

4. Let sit 2 minutes.

5. Devour!

Katie C. - Forest Grove, OR, US

Section Hiker | Supporter-Follower | 2011 to 2015

Mile 566.5 – Kohnen Bakery in Tehachapi, California with Pop-Top, Karaoke and Juniper

Mile 151.9 - Paradise Valley Cafe, Mountain Center, California
Little Miss Wonderful (behind us, serving other hiker trash)
Back Row (L to R): Rainman, Dundee, Narwhal
Front Row (L to R): Speedy Gonzales, Wall Street and Snow White

Omnivorous Dishes

Mile 296.0 – Holcomb Crossing in the San Bernadino Mountains, California

Alaska Spamwich

This recipe honors 2 Alaskan food groups, Pilot Bread and Spam brand meat.

Best for **Lunch**

Servings: **1**	Calories: 410	Protein (g): 9	Carbs (g): 36

Requires At-Home Prep: **No**
Prep Time: **none**
Cook Time: **none**

On-Trail Prep Time: **1 minute**
Cook Time: **none**

2 Sailor Boy brand Pilot Bread crackers

1 package Hormel brand Spam Single Classic

Instructions:

1. Open Spam brand packet.

2. Squeeze contents onto 1 Pilot Bread cracker.

3. Cover with second cracker.

4. Enjoy this quick, delicious and high cal trail lunch!

www.Alisonsterley.wordpress.com

Alison "Catwater" S. - Anchorage, AK, US

Thru Hiker | 2015

Image Credit: Alison Sterley

Asian Chicken Salad

When you crave a cool green salad this will satisfy your cravings! Minimus sells individual shelf stable salad dressings that add a lot of fat and calories to this recipe.

Best for **Lunch**

Servings: **1**

Requires At-Home Prep:	**Yes**	On-Trail Prep Time:	**5 minutes**
Prep Time:	**10 minutes**	Cook Time:	**none**
Cook Time:	**none**		

Sources for ingredients:

Minimus: Individual packages of shelf stable salad dressing and olive oil
http://www.minimus.biz/

Packit Gourmet: smaller packages of freeze dried meats, cheese, salad dressing
http://www.packitgourmet.com/

Bulk #10 cans of freeze dried meats, vegetables and fruits:

> *http://shop.honeyville.com/*

> *http://www.thrivelife.com/shop*

> *http://www.harmonyhousefoods.com/*

1/4 cup Harmony House brand dried cabbage

1/4 package ramen crushed

1/4 packet ramen seasoning

1/3 cup freeze dried chicken

1/4 cup freeze dried peas

1 tsp dried green onions or chives

1/4 cup sliced almonds

1 packet Chelten House brand Organic Sesame Ginger Dressing

Instructions:

1. Place the first 6 ingredients into a pint Ziploc brand freezer bag.

2. Place the individual salad dressing packet and almonds into snack size baggie and place baggie in with other salad ingredients.

3. An hour before lunch remove the almond and salad dressing packet from salad mixture and add cold water just to cover ingredients. Seal Ziploc brand bag well.

4. At lunch time squeeze out any excess water, add salad dressing and almonds to salad mixture and stir together.

Judy "Plan B" F. - Issaquah, WA, US

Section Hiker | 2005 to 2015

Breakfast For Dinner

Because it's just too darn hard to do dishes in the morning.

Best for **Dinner**

Servings: **1**

Requires At-Home Prep:	**Maybe**
Prep Time:	none
Cook Time:	none
On-Trail Prep Time:	**15 min to 2 hours**, depending on if you soak dehydrated veggies
Cook Time:	**5 to 20 minutes** (depending on if you use dehydrated veggies)

Create measuring lines on the tools you have before you go. For example, measure 1/4 c., 1/3 c., 1/2 c., 1 c. etc. on the outside of a see through water bottle. Make a small notch in your plastic utensil to indicate the level of a tsp. and tbsp.

1/2 cup Ova Easy brand egg crystals

2/3 cup water

1 tbsp powdered butter, adjust to taste or use oil to coat pot

powdered cheese, qty at your discretion; whisk with dehydrated milk, butter, or water

dehydrated/dried veggies, your choice of tomatoes, onion, garlic, etc.

spices, your choice of red pepper flakes, salt, pepper, hot sauce, etc.

1 summer sausage, sliced

tortillas, on the side or to make a wrap

Instructions:

1. If rehydrating veggies, do that first. Generally a 1:2 ratio of veggies:water on a 10-15 minute simmer or 1-2 hour soak.

2. Slice sausage while you wait.

3. Whisk butter with 1/2 tsp of water (or use oil) in your cup or bowl; pour in pot and heat and coat pot.

4. Whisk eggs with 2/3 cup water in your cup or bowl; pour in pot and stir.

5. Whisk cheese either in cup or bowl or add directly to cooking eggs.

6. Add veggies to cooking eggs.

7. Add spices either while cooking or after cooking. If you accidentally grab a few extra packets at fast food restaurants you can end up with quite the collection

8. Do what you will with your tortilla!

Use on the side or to make a wrap.

Tears S. - Roselle Park, NJ, US

Family-Friend | 2015

Breakfast Rice

Warm and comforting like my mothers rice pudding. This will take at least 15 minutes in a cozy or your hat to completely reconstitute the rice . Alternately make it when you are breaking camp and carry it with you for morning break.

Best for **Breakfast**

Servings: **1**

Requires At-Home Prep:	**Yes**	On-Trail Prep Time:	**5 minutes**
Prep Time:	**10 minutes**	Cook Time:	**15 minutes sitting**
Cook Time:	**none**		

Coconut cream powder and vanilla powder are found in Asian markets or online.

Nido brand is full fat dried milk found in Asian markets or in the hispanic section of many grocery stores.

1/2 cup instant rice

1/4 tsp cinnamon

1/4 cup raisins

1/4 cup pecans, chopped

2 tbsp Nido brand powdered milk

2 tbsp coconut cream powder

1 tbsp brown sugar

1 tsp vanilla sugar

1 tsp potato starch, can be omitted but it helps thicken

Instructions:

1. At home place all ingredients into a pint freezer bag.

2. On trail add 1+ cup boiling water and let sit in cozy a full 15 minutes.

3. Stir and add more boiling water if needed.

Judy "Plan B" F. - Issaquah, WA, US

Calorie Sandwich

I first made this on the Devil's Dome Loop trail and didn't have much food in my fridge, but most of which would go bad by the time I got back! The thing I craved most on previous trips was bacon and high calorie foods that weren't plain old processed bars. It tastes like cheesy bacony goodness, because, well, that's all it is! I personally hike with a very heavy pack so I rarely hike with dehydrated meals, so if you're a UL this might not be up your alley.

Best for **Breakfast | Dinner**

Servings: **1**   Calories: 590   Protein (g): 19   Carbs (g): 48

Requires At-Home Prep:	**Maybe**	On-Trail Prep Time:	**2 minutes**
Prep Time:	**1 minute**	Cook Time:	**5 to 7 minutes**
Cook Time:	**5 to 10 minutes**		

Cook the bacon before you set out, so this is ideal if you stop in town at a hotel with a mini kitchen, somewhere that allows campfires, or somewhere you can buy more fuel.
Cured/smoked bacon is the best so it has little chance of going bad in your bag, especially after being cooked. For the bread I usually buy one of those $1-$2 loaves of french bread because you can squish it to save room, then cut off large sections (~5 per loaf) and turn it into a "pita" by opening up the middle. Choose cheese that stays firm without refrigeration

1/5 loaf french bread   **3 strips** bacon, pre-cooked   **1/2 cup** cheese

Instructions:

1. Reheat the bacon to kill any food borne illness.

2. Add cheese to cooking pan with bacon until melted.

3. Put mixture onto/into bread and enjoy!

Katherine I. - Bothell, WA, US

Supporter-Follower | 2014 to 2015

Carrot Apple Raisin Salad

The bacon bits can be left out for vegetarian option.

Best for **Lunch**

Servings: **1**

Requires At-Home Prep:	Yes	On-Trail Prep Time:	**5 minutes**
Prep Time:	**10 minutes**	Cook Time:	**none**
Cook Time:	**6 hours to dehydrate carrots**		

Dehydrate carrots: Shred carrots then blanch by pouring boiling water over carrots. Drain and blot dry then dry in dehydrator about 6 hours.

Source for individual packages of shelf stable salad dressing: http://www.minimus.biz/

1/2 cup dried shredded carrot

2 tbsp dried apples, chopped

2 tbsp raisins

2 tbsp shelf stable bacon bits

1/4 package ramen, crushed

1/4 cup roasted cashews

1 packet Chelten House brand Organic Sesame Ginger dressing

Instructions:

1. Place the first 5 ingredients into a pint Ziploc brand freezer bag.

2. Place the individual salad dressing packet and cashews into snack size baggie and place baggie in with other salad ingredients.

3. In the morning on the trail remove the cashew and salad dressing packet from salad mixture and add cold water just to cover ingredients. Seal Ziploc brand bag well.

4. At lunch time squeeze out any excess water, add salad dressing and cashews to salad mixture and stir together.

Judy "Plan B" F. - Issaquah, WA, US

Section Hiker | 2005 to 2015

Cheesy Beef and Rice

This is one of those comfort foods at the end of a hard day.

Best for **Dinner**

Servings: **1**   Calories: 760

Requires At-Home Prep:	**Yes**
Prep Time:	10 minutes, unless you make your own rice or hamburger
Cook Time:	30 minutes for rice or hamburger + 8 hours of dehydrating time
On-Trail Prep Time:	5 minutes to boil water
Cook Time:	20 minutes sitting in cozy or pot

Let it sit a full 20 minutes and keep hot in a cozy or your pot otherwise you will have crunchy rice. I like to get dried fried scallions at the Asian market but those french fried onion for green bean casserole may be easier to find.

1 cup instant rice, see alternate to make your own instant rice

1/2 package Knorr brand 4-Cheese sauce mix

1/4 cup freeze dried beef, see alternate to make your own dried beef

1/4 cup freeze dried peas

2 tbsp french fried onions

1/4 cup Nido brand dried milk

2 tbsp Kraft brand parmesan cheese, shelf stable

1-1/2+ cups boiling water

25

Instructions:

1. Place all ingredients into a freezer bag or vacuum bag at home.

2. Add 1-1/2+ cups of boiling water to freezer bag or add mix to boiling water in pot.

3. Let sit at least 20 minutes.

Alternate preparation:

RICE: To make instant rice I like to use brown Jasmine rice.

1. Place 1 cup of rice in a heavy pan and toast until it pops like popcorn.

2. Add 2 cups of water and simmer until all water is gone.

3. Place rice on dehydrator tray and dry completely.

4. Roll rice in towel until well broken up. Use in place of instant rice.

HAMBURGER:

1. Cook lean organic ground beef completely, breaking up into small pieces.

2. Put hamburger into sieve and rinse with hot water to remove fat.

3. Dry well in dehydrator.

Judy "Plan B" F. - Issaquah, WA, US

Section Hiker | 2005 to 2015

Chicken Spiral Alfredo with Asparagus

I was looking for a dinner for a last minute trip. On my PCT section hike, one of the meals was supposed to have asparagus. I was so tired from the long day, I forgot to add the asparagus. So I needed to come up with something to use asparagus in. I knew, I had some already dehydrated noodles and chicken, as well as Alfredo sauce on the pantry shelf. Since I dehydrate those in large batches. This recipe was the result. I made it for the first time October 4, 2015 on the Forsyth Trail in Pine Valley, UT. Tasted just like I made it in the pot at home. Yummy!

Best for **Lunch | Dinner**

Servings: **1**

Requires At-Home Prep:	**Yes**	On-Trail Prep Time:	**30 minutes**
Prep Time:	**1 hour**	Cook Time:	**20 minutes**
Cook Time:	**20 hours**		

I always do large batches of canned chicken, must be canned in order to rehydrate right, as well as large batches of vegetables and noodles so I have quick dinner ingredients for last minute trips. You can double this recipe for a larger serving size or two people. You can remove the chicken for a meat free meal.

1 cup Renzoni brand Garden Delight Spiral Noodles, cooked according to package

1/2 cup canned chicken breast

1 cup fresh asparagus or broccoli, lightly steamed

1 packet olive oil

1/2 packet Knorr brand Alfredo Sauce, weigh out at 7/8 ounces in a zip top sandwich bag

3-1/2 tbsp Nido brand powdered milk

1 packet salt and pepper, to taste

Image Credit: Jodi Knight

Instructions:

At home:

1. Measure out 1/2 cup servings of canned chicken; spread out on dehydrator trays.

2. Dehydrate for 12 hours on 155° F. Dehydrating times vary for the humidity in your area. Chicken should be completely dry without signs of moisture. It is possible that you may need to leave it in longer than 12 hours.

3. With a Sharpie brand pen, write the measurements on the storage container.

4. Once the chicken is dehydrated, let cool completely.

5. Once cooled, add to pre-marked storage containers.

6. Measure out 1 cup of precooked noodles; spread out on dehydrator trays.

7. Measure out 1 cup of steamed asparagus-broccoli; spread out on dehydrator trays.

8. Dehydrate noodles and veggies on 125° F for 8 hours.

9. With a Sharpie brand pen, write the measurements on the storage container.

10. Once the noodles and veggies are dehydrated, let cool completely.

11. Once cooled, add to pre-marked containers.

In Camp:

1. Open the chicken, make sure it has not gone rancid.

2. About 30 minutes prior to cooking time, add enough water to the chicken and asparagus-broccoli to measure 1-1/2 cups. Let soak to rehydrate. I do this while I set up camp.

3. Add enough water to the noodles to make 1 cup; add to your pan and heat on low setting, until noodles are soft. Approximately 5 minutes.

4. Drain any excess water off of chicken and asparagus-broccoli.

5. Drain any excess water off of the noodles.

6. Add chicken and asparagus to the noodles in the pan.

7. Measure out just a little over 3/4 cup of water.

8. Add oil packet to the pan.

9. Add the alfredo sauce mix to the pan.

10. Add the Nido brand powdered milk to the pan.

11. Add a little over 3/4 cup of water to the pan.

12. Turn heat up to medium, stirring frequently until done; approximately 10 minutes.

13. Add salt and pepper to taste. I only use 1 pepper packet.

14. Kick back and enjoy your homemade meal!

https://journeysofsnakejumper.wordpress.com

Jodi "Snake Jumper" K. - Las Vegas, NV, US

Section Hiker | 2015

Shellfish Free | Nut Free | Egg Free

Chili-Cheese-Mash-Mac Wraps

A delicious take on chili cheese fries, backcountry style! Chili and cheese come together with mashed potatoes. Served burrito style with little to no clean up after!

Best for **Lunch | Dinner**

Servings: 2

Requires At-Home Prep: **No**

Prep Time: **none**

Cook Time: **none**

On-Trail Prep Time: **2 to 5 minutes**

Cook Time: **10 to 15 minutes**

Add a little oil for extra calories!

1 bag Mountain House brand Chili Mac with Beef, cook according to directions on box with 3-4 extra ounces of water for potatoes AFTER adding other ingredients

1/2 bag Idahoan brand 4 Cheese OR Garlic mashed potatoes, add to Mountain House brand meal before adding boiling water

1-2 tsp chili powder, optional; add to potato and chili mixture

1-2 tsp cumin, optional; add to potato and chili mixture

1-2 cloves garlic, chopped, optional; add to other ingredients

4 slices cheddar cheese, optional; top with mixture after stirring in boiling water so it can melt as it sits

4 whole flour tortillas, fill with mixture when done, wrap like a burrito, and enjoy

Instructions:

1. Boil 15 to 16 ounces of water.

2. While water is boiling, remove the oxygen absorber from the Mountain House brand chili mac and add your half bag of potatoes and any of the optional seasonings.

3. Add boiling water to Mountain House brand bag mixture, and stir well.

4. Place cheese slices on top and close bag to let sit as per Mountain House brand instructions.

5. Spoon mixture into tortillas as desired and enjoy!

www.Takebothroads.wordpress.com

Rachael "Chef" H. - Corning, CA US

Nataniel "Vulture" M.

Thru Hiker | Family-Friend | Supporter-Follower | 2015

Thru Hiker | 2015

Image Credit: Charles "Foolish" M.

Foolish Lentil Stew

Ancient Roman Army recipe

Best for **Dinner**

Servings: **1**

Requires At-Home Prep: **No**
Prep Time: **none**
Cook Time: **none**

On-Trail Prep Time: **5 minutes, max**
Cook Time: **5 minutes**

sprouted green lentils

bacon bits

olive oil

Craisin brand dried cranberries

salt, tumeric, cumin, to taste

French fries or onion rings

instant rice

Instructions:

1. Soak Lentils at noon.

2. Heat, boil briefly, add everything else in one pot.

3. Add instant rice at end.

Charles "Foolish" M. - Houston, TX, US

Thru Hiker | Trail Angel | 2015

Get Your Groove On Granola

Pre make at home granola that you can take with you on the trail or while you are hiking!

Best for **Snack**

Servings: **12**

Requires At-Home Prep:	**Yes**	On-Trail Prep Time:	**none**
Prep Time:	**15 minutes**	Cook Time:	**none**
Cook Time:	**30 to 50 minutes**		

4 cups oats

2 tbsp canola oil

1/2 cup maple syrup

1/2 cup honey

1/2 tsp sea salt

1-1/2 cups of any...nuts, dried fruit, seeds, shredded coconut, nut butters

Instructions:

1. Preheat oven to 280° F.

2. In large bowl add oats and oil; stir.

3. In a small pot over stove, melt syrup and honey; add salt and nut butters; stir.

4. You can add a bit more syrup and/or honey if you like it sweeter!!

5. You can also add some brown sugar!!

6. Pour syrup mixture over oats.

7. Add any nuts or seeds you are using, stir.

8. Grease 1 large cookie tray and spread mixture over it.

9. Bake 30-50 minutes, stirring batch a couple of times while cooking.

10. Granola is done when golden brown.

11. Add any dried fruit after you turn off your oven and leave the tray in the oven to cool!!

12. After granola has cooled put in a Ziploc brand bag and you are good to go!! Enjoy!!

Denise "Tree Huggin' Girl!" C. - Garden Grove, CA, US

Section Hiker | 2012 to 2015

Hiker Hunger Hot Dogs

As Thru-Hikers are always talking about food, a challenge of sorts was hatched for Kennedy Meadows. As I was already carrying peanut butter and tortillas, the object of the challenge was to pick up something from the Kennedy Meadows General Store to add to those two items.

Best for **Lunch | Dinner | Snack**

Servings: **1**

Requires At-Home Prep:	**No**
Prep Time:	**none**
Cook Time:	**none**
On-Trail Prep Time:	**5 minutes**
Cook Time:	**10 minutes**

Be creative. There are four basic items, but so many more could be added according to taste or daring.

1 tortilla

2 tbsp peanut butter, creamy or chunky - your choice

1 hot dog, cooked over open flame

hot sauce, as much or as little as you like

Optional items as desired

Instructions:

1. Cook hot dog over open flame; campfire preferred, where safe and legal to do so.

2. Lay out tortilla.

3. Spread 2 tbsp of peanut butter on one half of the tortilla.

4. Place cooked hot dog on the peanut butter side of tortilla.

5. Add hot sauce and/or other optional items.

6. Roll up tortilla like a burrito.

7. Enjoy & repeat.

http://quixotethruhiker.weebly.com/

Tom "Quixote" S. - Auke Bay, AK, US

Thru Hiker | 2015

Shellfish Free | Nut Free

Mac-n-Cheese with Chili-n-Chicken

I love chili and I love macaroni and cheese. This recipe uses all instant-type, pre-packaged and dehydrated foods, so there's very little at-home prep.

Best for **Lunch | Dinner**

Servings: **1 to 2**   Calories: **1150**   Protein (g): **95**   Carbs (g): **165**

Requires At-Home Prep: **Yes**   On-Trail Prep Time: **none**
Prep Time: **5 minutes**   Cook Time: **15 to 20 minutes**
Cook Time: **none**

A little at-home prep (sorting and re-bagging ingredients and writing basic instructions) will help you reduce weight and allow you to cook faster while you're on trail.

7.25 oz box Kraft brand Macaroni-n-Cheese

1/3 packet Carroll Shelby brand's Orginal Texas Chili Kit

1 heaping tbsp Peak Dry Whole Milk Powder

4 tbsp Hoosier Hill Farm brand Butter Blend powder

7 oz pouch Tyson brand Premium Chunk White Chicken

1 large pinch Harmony House brand Foods Dried Diced Tomatoes

1 large pinch Harmony House brand Foods True Dehydrated Dark Kidney Beans

Instructions:

At home:

1. Obtain a quart-sized Ziploc brand freezer bag and a Ziploc brand snack-sized bag.

2. With a Sharpie brand pen, write "3 cups, 10 min" on the outside of the freezer bag.

3. Place the macaroni noodles, tomatoes and kidney beans into a quart-sized Ziploc brand freezer bag.

4. In the snack-sized bag, dump in the cheese mix; then measure out and add the chili mix, milk powder and butter powder.

On the trail:

5. Hike 20-30 miles.

6. Add macaroni, tomatoes and kidney beans to 3 cups of water in your cooking pot.

7. Bring to a boil and then simmer for 10 minutes.

8. Add chicken during last minute.

9. Turn off flame. Add powder mix and stir thoroughly. Eat well.

www.cookingonthepct.com

Martin "Rainman" L. - San Diego, CA, US   Section Hiker | Trail Angel | Family-Friend | Supporter-Follower | 2015

Mexi Bean Salad

There is some up front preparation with the dehydration of the beans and macaroni but this is a good project for the wet cold months while you are planning for the trail. Both the beans and macaroni will last a year if kept from moisture and in the dark. Precooking and drying macaroni allows it to be reconstituted with cold water.

Best for **Lunch**

Servings: **1**

Requires At-Home Prep:	**Yes**	On-Trail Prep Time:	**5 minutes**
Prep Time:	**10 minutes**	Cook Time:	**none**
Cook Time:	**8 hours for dehydration**		

Dehydrating:

Beans: Rinse canned beans well then spread on dehydrator trays. Dry until beans pop open about 6-8 hours at about 125° F.

Macaroni: Cook small salad macaroni about 7-9 minutes. Rinse with cold water and then spread on dehydrator trays. Dry about 8 hours.

Sources for Salad dressing:

Individual packages of shelf stable ranch salad dressing: http://www.minimus.biz/

Alternate: Hidden Valley brand Ranch dressing in individual containers in many grocery stores.

1/4 cup dehydrated kidney beans

1/4 cup dehydrated black beans

1/4 cup dehydrated garbanzo beans

1/4 cup freeze dried corn

1 tsp dried parsley

1 tsp dried cilantro

1 tbsp sun dried tomatoes, chopped fine

2 tsp chili powder

1 tsp cumin

2 tsp onion flakes

2 tbsp sunflower seeds

1/4 cup salad macaroni. cooked and dried

1 packet Chelton House Organic Ranch dressing

Instructions:

1. Place all ingredients in a pint freezer bag.

2. Place the salad dressing packet in with salad ingredients.

3. In the morning on the trail remove the salad dressing packet from the freezer bag then just cover the "salad" with cold water.

4. Reseal the freezer bag carefully.

5. At lunch time drain any excess water from salad and mix in the salad dressing.

Judy "Plan B" F. - Issaquah, WA, US

Michelin Potato

Ramen with a twist

Best for **Lunch | Dinner**

Servings: **1**

Requires At-Home Prep:	**No**	On-Trail Prep Time:	**4 minutes**
Prep Time:	**none**	Cook Time:	**4 minutes**
Cook Time:	**none**		

Make sure you add plenty of water.

1/2 packet dried potato with garlic

1 packet your favourite ramen

chili flakes

water

boil-in-the-bag

Instructions:

1. Boil water

2. In the meantime, put the potato, ramen and chili flakes into a boil-in-the-bag.

3. When the water is boiled, add to the boil-in-the-bag contents.

4. Stir, or if your hands are cold, "squeeze" the bag to mix.

5. Leave for 1 minute.

6. Eat, relax and enjoy the views knowing that you have been let off the washing up this evening!

Adaptations: choose different flavours of ramen or use potato with four cheeses.

www.Emmakelty.blogspot.com

Emma "Fosters" K. - Surrey, England, United Kingdom   Thru Hiker | 2015

Protein Packed Spaghetti

By using Barilla brand Protein Plus and turkey sausage in this recipe, you amp up the protein to about 27 grams per serving. You can also omit the turkey sausage for a vegetarian meal. I started dehydrating my own meals, because I like to know what is in my food and to lighten my pack. Those "bagged" foods are just heavy and tasteless. And whats really in them? The first go at this recipe was on the Whipple Trail in Utah. I used several friends as taste testers, it was a hit and the pot was empty, so I added it to my PCT Section hike trip meal plan.

Best for **Lunch | Dinner**

Servings: **1**   Protein (g): 27

Requires At-Home Prep:	**Yes**	On-Trail Prep Time: **30 to 45 minutes**
Prep Time:	**30 minutes**	Cook Time: **10 to 15 minutes**
Cook Time:	**21 hours**	

I start the reconstitution process for the meat (if you're using the meat) as soon as I get to camping location, or even at the lunch stop, so that it's rehydrated when your ready for dinner. I also keep the meat separate from the sauce/noodles, just in case the meat goes rancid, then everything is not ruined. I use the bread crumbs to help the sausage re-hydrate better. I write the measurements on the bags with a Sharpie brand, as well as the instructions so that I do not forget in camp. If you use the fruit roll up trays, the tomato sauce will discolor your trays, but they are still usable and my fruit roll ups did not taste like spaghetti.

15.2 oz package Barilla brand Protein Plus spaghetti noodles, cook according to directions

1 tsp olive oil

19.5 oz package Jenny-O brand Sweet Italian Turkey Sausage, casings removed

1/2 cup Italian bread crumbs

Image Credit: Jodi "Snake Jumper" Knight

1/2 tbsp olive oil

2 large bell peppers, diced

1 small yellow onion, diced

8 oz package fresh mushrooms, diced

15 oz can diced tomatoes

15 oz can tomato sauce

6 oz can tomato paste

1 tsp garlic salt, or to taste

1 tsp basil, or to taste

Instructions:

At home:

1. Following the instructions on the Barilla brand Protein Plus package, cook the spaghetti noodles adding 1 tsp of olive oil to the water.

2. Once cooked, drain noodles and run cold water over the noodles to keep them from sticking. Set aside.

3. While the noodles are cooking, in a medium sized bowl, remove and throw away the casing from the turkey sausage. Mix the turkey sausage with the Italian bread crumbs.

4. In a large skillet, thoroughly cook the turkey sausage, on a medium heat, keeping it separate from the other ingredients.

5. Heat the 1/2 tbsp of olive oil in a large pot.

6. Add the diced bell peppers, onions and mushrooms and saute on a medium heat in the oil until tender.

7. Add the diced tomatoes, tomato sauce and tomato paste and spices to the vegetables, mix and turn down the heat to low and allow to cook for about an hour, stirring frequently.

8. Mix the noodles and the sauce together, enjoy a nice spaghetti dinner. I recommend a good glass of Merlot to pair with it.

9. Let the leftovers cool down.

10. Get out your dehydrator.

11. Measure 1 cup of the sauce and noodle mix per person serving.

12. Spread the sauce and noodle mix evenly on your dehydrator tray, using either parchment paper or the solid fruit roll up trays, using 1 tray per each trail dinner/lunch.

13. Measure 1/4 cup of the turkey sausage per one person serving.

14. Spread the turkey sausage on a separate tray, using 1 tray per trail dinner/lunch.

15. With a Sharpie brand pen write on your storage container, what the original measurement was for each trail dinner/lunch.

16. Let dehydrate for approximately 20 hours at 135° F. Dehydration time may vary depending on the humidity in your area. There should be no moisture or wetness left when your food is completely dehydrated.

17. Store in Ziploc brand or vacuum sealed bags. Keep the meat separate from the sauce and noodle mix.

On the trail:

1. Check the turkey meat to make sure it has not gone rancid. It should still be dry and have no sign of moisture.

2. About 30-45 mins prior to dinner time, add in enough water to the turkey sausage to make the original serving size, so if the original serving was 1/4 cup, put the meat into your bowl and add enough water to the bowl to measure 1/4 cup.

3. Let the meat stand and reconstitute while you set up camp.

4. About 5 minutes prior to dinner time, add the sausage to your pan.

5. In your bowl, put the sauce and noodle mix, adding enough water to make the original serving size, same as the meat.

6. Let the sauce and noodle mix stand until soft, approximately 5 minutes.

7. Once the sauce and noodle mix has softened, add it to the cooking pan with the turkey meat and cook on low setting until done, approximately 10-15 minutes.

8. Put your feet up, soak in your amazing view and enjoy your flavorful home cooked meal, while your camp mates add water to a bag and hope it's not crunchy or watery. Maybe even share some, if you make a double serving.

https://journeysofsnakejumper.wordpress.com/

Jodi "Snake Jumper" K. - Las Vegas, NV, US

Shepherd's Chicken Pie

This is more or less a Shepherd's Pie Recipe made with instant potatoes, a Knorr brand Pasta Side dish and a bag or can of chicken.

Best for **Dinner**

| Servings: **1** | Calories: 440 | Protein (g): 22 | Carbs (g): 63 |

Requires At-Home Prep:	**No**	On-Trail Prep Time:	none
Prep Time:	**none**	Cook Time:	**10 minutes**
Cook Time:	**none**		

You can add any fresh vegetables you want to change it up some.

1/2 package Idahoan brand Buttery Homestyle potatoes

1/2 bag Knorr brand Sides Chicken Flavor

4.5 oz can Swanson brand chicken

Instructions:

1. Bring water to a boil and add noodles. Add the chicken after 4 minutes, then cook for another 3 minutes.

2. When the noodles and chicken are done, let them sit for 3 minutes. In this time, boil the water for the potatoes. Mix in the potatoes and let sit for 1 minute.

3. When all ingredients are cooked, mix them together and enjoy.

Rob "Bear Ka-Rob" S. - Las Vegas, NV, US   Trail Angel | Family-Friend | 2013 to 2015

Shepherd's Pie

Taking time to make the potatoes separate from the gravy makes this feel like a real meal. So warm on a wet cold day.

Best for **Dinner**

Servings: **1**

Requires At-Home Prep:**Yes**	On-Trail Prep Time: **5 minutes**
Prep Time: **10 minutes**	Cook Time: **15 minutes sitting**
Cook Time: **none**	

Make the instant potatoes directly in your mug and just keep pouring the gravy over them as you eat it down! Saves using 2 freezer bags.

1/4 cup freeze dried or dehydrated ground beef

1/2 package brown gravy mix

1/8 cup *each* freeze dried: peas, corn, green beans

1/8 cup dehydrated carrots

1/4 cup dried mushrooms

1 tbsp French's brand fried dried onions

1/2 package Idahoan brand instant potatoes

Instructions:

1. This recipes is made in 2 freezer bags. One for potatoes and one for gravy.

2. Place all ingredients except potatoes in one freezer bag. Place instant potatoes in separate bag.

4. On trail boil water and add 1 cup boiling water to gravy mix.

5. Add 1 cup boiling water to potatoes. Let both bags sit 15 minutes.

7. Mix gravy vegetable mixture and pour over potatoes.

Judy "Plan B" F. - Issaquah, WA, US   Section Hiker | 2005 to 2015

Silly Momo PB Ramen

This is so good and refreshing in hot or cold weather. Add 2 packets of spicey ramen to boiling water (about 700 ml, or to taste). Then add two packets of Justin's brand peanut butter and mix together. You can add dehydrated meat or vegetables if you have it, or just leave it plain. Let simmer for 1 minute until noodles are cooked and texture is creamy.

Best for **Lunch | Dinner**

Servings: **2**   Calories: **570**   Protein (g): **16**   Carbs (g): **57**

Requires At-Home Prep: **No**   On-Trail Prep Time: **1 minute**
Prep Time: **none**   Cook Time: **3 minutes**
Cook Time: **none**

This recipe is a good way to consume extra calories from peanut butter without the sticky texture. We altered this recipe with dehydrated bean sprouts, garlic, and pine nuts to make a pseudo Thai dish on the trail.

2 packets spicy ramen, follow package instructions   **2-4 cups** water, to taste; use according to ramen instructions
2 Justin's brand peanut butter packets

Instructions:

1. Bring water to boil

2. Add peanut butter Stir. Let simmer

3. Add ingredients to taste (dehydrated veggies, spices, nuts).

4. Enjoy.

Jennifer T. - Glendale, AZ, US   Thru Hiker | 2016
Morgan J.   Thru Hiker | 2016

Slammin Salmon Terra Gone

Salmon and asparagus with tarragon beurre blanc on brown rice.

Best for **Dinner**

Servings: **1**   Calories: **2000**

Requires At-Home Prep: **Yes**   On-Trail Prep Time: **5 minutes**
Prep Time: **15 minutes**   Cook Time: **5 minutes**
Cook Time: **10 minutes plus 2 hours of drying**

Instead of just poaching the salmon, if you are prepared for cooking other fish, you can sear it or bake in foil, whatever you plan to do with those trout.

12 oz fresh salmon, dry in Excalibur brand dehydrator or similar to firm but not leathery

2 boil-bags Success brand brown rice, mix with asparagus

8 oz asparagus, dehydrated

2 tbsp powdered butter

1 pinch salt

2 pinches powdered garlic

1+ tbsp dried tarragon

1 Ziploc brand bag or vac pack

Instructions:

1. At last rest stop before dinner, cover salmon in water in zip lock or wide mouth bottle.

2. At camp, cover rice/asparagus mix with water; set salmon on top and add olive oil, ghee, coconut oil, mac nuts, almonds, etc. to taste

3. Cover. Boil. Barely.

4. Let stand till cooled to taste, 10 minutes or so. Mow it.

Peter H. - Pinecliffe, CO, US

Spaghetti Carbonara

So you're on the trail, and there's no Italian restaurant to be found. Suddenly, you reach in your Ursack brand sack and pull out the quart-size Ziploc brand bag of Creamy Cheesy Bacon-y Goodness. Problem Solved!

Best for **Dinner**

Servings: **1**

Requires At-Home Prep:	**Yes**	On-Trail Prep Time:	**5 minutes**
Prep Time:	**10 minutes**	Cook Time:	**10 minutes**
Cook Time:	**Dehydration time (will vary, but is easy to do)**		

Even shelf-stable bacon can go rancid in the heat. You can skip the bacon if you'd like, or just vacuum seal into a tiny bag. Play it smart, and if it smells "off," just pitch it.

4 oz dehydrated spaghetti, add to quart zip-top bag

1/4 cup Kraft brand parmesan cheese, add to snack bag #1

1/2 tbsp dry oregano, add to snack bag #1

1/4 tsp finely ground black pepper, add to snack bag #1

2 tbsp Ova Easy brand egg crystals add to sandwich bag

2 packets extra virgin olive oil

3/4 oz (by weight) shelf stable chopped bacon, add to snack bag #2 OR vacuum seal into small bag

Instructions:

At home:

1. If you have a dehydrator, cook spaghetti until not quite al dente. Dehydrate in 4 oz portions.

2. Place snack bag #1 (cheese/spices), snack bag #2 (or vacuum sealed bag), sandwich bag (Ova Easy brand egg crystals), olive oil packets, and 2 full sheets of paper towels (for cleanup), into the quart bag (which contains the dehydrated pasta).

3. Print the directions below, and add to quart bag.

On the trail:

4. Go hiking. Now. You need to get out of town.

5. Hike until you're famished and can't find that Italian restaurant.

6. Remove all of the individual bags/paper towels from the pasta bag.

7. Boil 2 cups water.

8. Add spaghetti to water, and cook for 1 minute before removing from heat. Put quart Ziploc brand into a cozy. Add spaghetti plus water to bag, and let sit for 5 minutes to finish rehydrating.(For non-dehydrated spaghetti, just cook until done, drain, and put in cozy).

10. Add 3 tbsp water to Ova Easy brand egg crystals sandwich bag. Seal and shake to dissolve. Set aside.

11. Add oil and bacon to (empty) pot. Cook over low heat until sizzling.

12. Drain spaghetti and add back into pot. Toss to combine.

13. Remove from heat.

14. Add egg mixture to pot and toss quickly (to avoid scrambling).

15. Add cheese mixture and toss.

16. Because this smells so awesome, violin players will appear and wander around the campsite, serenading you. If they're feeling benevolent, they'll serenade your buddy, who is woefully staring at his Top Ramen brand instant noodles.

www.lizfallin.wordpress.com

Liz "Rest Step" F. - Bothell, WA, US   Section Hiker | 2014 to 2015

*** *Rest Step is awesome! She was the first person to submit a recipe!* ***

Spanish Couscous

This is a take off on Spanish Rice but the couscous reconstitutes faster especially at high altitude. The meat can be freeze dried sausage or ground beef or home dehydrated ground beef.

Best for **Dinner**

Servings: **1**

Requires At-Home Prep:	**Yes**	On-Trail Prep Time:	**5 minutes**
Prep Time:	**8 hours for dehydration**	Cook Time:	**15 minutes sitting**
Cook Time:	**15 minutes for hamburger**		

Dehydration tips:

Spaghetti Sauce: Choose non-chunky style. Pour on parchment paper. Spread thinly and dry about 8 hours. Break up then grind in coffee grinder into fine powder. 1 large jar makes enough for 4 meals.

Black beans: Rinse canned black beans well then spread on dehydrator trays. Dry about 6 hours.

Red / yellow peppers: Choose the small sweet peppers. Wash then slice in 1/8 inch circles. Place on dehydrator trays and dry about 6 hours.

Ground beef: Choose very lean organic ground beef. Fry and break up into small pieces. Place cooked beef in sieve and rinse under hot tap water. Blot dry then dehydrate 8 hours at 135° F.

1/3 cup couscous

1/4 cup freeze dried or dehydrated ground beef or sausage

1/4 tsp dried onion

1/4 cup dried spagetti sauce powder

1/4 cup freeze dried corn

1/4 cup dried black beans

1 tbsp dried red or yellow peppers

1 tsp chili powder

1/2 tsp cumin

1/4 cup parmesan chees

Instructions:

1. Place all ingredients in 1 quart size Ziploc brand freezer bag.

2. On trail boil 1-1/2cups water and add to bag and stir.

3. Let sit in cozy 15 minutes then stir and enjoy!

Judy "Plan B" F. - Issaquah, WA, US

Section Hiker | 2005 to 2015

Image Credit: Shelly Skye

Stupendous Stroganoff

This is assembles without a packaged sauce and it's to die for yummy. I searched for a long time to find the ingredients so I could eat this meal without the chemicals found in prepackaged sauces.

Best for **Lunch | Dinner**

Servings: **1**

Requires At-Home Prep:	Yes
Prep Time:	5 minutes to assemble into Ziploc brand
Cook Time:	1 hour to cook turkey and pasta; 4 to 6 hours to dehydrate the ingredients
On-Trail Prep Time:	<1 minute to cover with water
Cook Time:	10 to 15 minutes sitting, plus boiling time

The recipe is for one serving but you can add and subtract at will.

1/2 cup bow tie or other pasta, cooked and dehydrated

1/3 cup low fat ground turkey, cooked, drained and dehydrated

2 tbsp dried mushrooms

1/2 tsp dried onions

1/2 tsp dry tarragon

1/8 tsp nutmeg

4 (or more) tbsp powdered sour cream

2 tsp powdered butter

salt and pepper to taste

Instructions:

1. Mix all together into one quart Ziploc brand bag and put into refrigerator until you are ready to go.

2. Salt and pepper to taste

3. Put water into Ziploc brand bag till just covering the goodies.

4. Wait for an hour or so till you find a great spot to stop and fire up the stove.

5. Put all into your pot and heat till it just starts to boil.

6. Remove from heat and put the pot into a cozy for 10 or 15 minutes. You are waiting for the ground turkey to rehydrate which takes longer than the pasta.

7. Eat and enjoy.

www.skyehiker.blogspot.com

Shelly "Topo" S. - Soquel, CA, US   Section Hiker | Trail Angel | Supporter-Follower | 2011 to 2015

Super Power Breakfast

As our favorite meal is breakfast, we were searching for an easy, delicious and super nutritious breakfast for the trail that we could send ourselves along the way. We just altered one of our normal oatmeal recipes- add lots of fat and protein.

Best for **Breakfast | Snack**

Servings: **2**

Requires At-Home Prep:	**Yes**	Cook Time:	**none**
Prep Time:	**2 days to soak nuts (to allow sprouting)**	On-Trail Prep Time:	**3 minutes to boil water**
	1 day to dry nuts, 2 minutes to assemble each bag	Cook Time:	**3 to 5 minutes soaking in boiling water**

Image Credit: Seth Conde

We combined all of the ingredients for each meal, put them in vacuum sealed bags and sent them to our resupply spots. All of the ingredient keep well in vacuum sealed bags. It's best if you have boiling water but it's possible to put cold water in it and let it soak for a while.

1-1/2 cups steel cut oats OR quick-rolled oats (steel cut have more fiber and calories but quick-rolled are easier)

1/4 (or more) cup brown sugar

1/2 (or more) cup sprouted chopped mixed nuts (almonds, walnuts, pecans, cashews, best if nuts are sprouted and then dried well to prevent them from rotting

2 tbsp chia seeds

1 tbsp hemp seeds

1 tsp flax seeds

2 scoops amazing grass green superfood, chocolate is the best flavor

2 tbsp dried coconut milk powder, can find it cheap in Asian markets

Optional ingredients to add: raisins, powdered peanut butter, chocolate chipsInstructions:

At home:

1. Put all ingredients in vacuum sealer bags- in any order

On trail:

2. Boil water.

3. Put all ingredients in a bowl; pour hot water over until food is covered in water.

4. Let it sit 3-5 minutes. Enjoy!

Option: can just add cold water, close container, hike for a while and then eat instead of boiling. But must use quick rolled oats then.

www.Alovegonewild.blogspot.com

Amy "Glitter Bug" B. - Portland, OR, US
Seth "Boombox" C.

Thru Hiker | Section Hiker | 2014
Thru Hiker | 2014

Thanksgiving In A Bag

Turns instant stuffing mix into a complete meal. This is a freezer bag just add water meal.

Best for **Dinner**

Servings: **1**

Requires At-Home Prep:	**Yes**	On-Trail Prep Time:	**5 minutes**
Prep Time:	**10 minutes**	Cook Time:	**15 minutes sitting**
Cook Time:	**none**		

1/2 box stuffing mix, either bread or cornbread stuffing

1/4 cup Craisin brand dried cranberries

1/4 cup freeze dried corn

1/4 cup freeze dried chicken

1/4 cup cashews

Alternate: 3 oz package or tin chicken

Instructions:

1. Package all ingredients into Ziploc brand brand 1 quart freezer bag.

2. On trail boil water and add 1-1/2 C boiling water to bag and stir to mix.

3. Let sit 15 minutes in cozy.

Alternate:

1. Boil 1-1/2 cups water and add contents of bag directly to pot.

2. Cover and let sit 15 minutes.

Judy "Plan B" F. - Issaquah, WA, US

Section Hiker | 2005 to 2015

Mile 104.5 – San Jose Del Valle near Cañada Buena Vista, California

The Official Sonora Pass Cafe Cookie

The world-famous cookie served at Sonora Pass.

Best for **Dessert**

Servings: **1**

Requires At-Home Prep:	No	On-Trail Prep Time:	**15 seconds**
Prep Time:	none	Cook Time:	none
Cook Time:	none		

1 large Costco brand Gourmet Chocolate Chip cookie

1 can extra creamy whipped cream

1 fresh red cherry

Instructions:

1. Smother cookie with as much whipped cream as possible.

2. Place fresh cherry on top.

http://ww2.kqed.org/news/2014/10/05/pacific-crest-trail-hikers-find-refuge-at-the-sonora-pass-café

Hank "The Owl" M. - Palo Alto, CA, US

Trail Angel | Supporter-Follower | 2004 to 2015

Image Credit: Patches, https://resonantliving. wordpress.com/tag/ sonora-pass-cafe/

Trail Pizza

As close to a pizza as you can get away from town

Best for **Lunch | Dinner**

Servings: **1**

Requires At-Home Prep:	**Yes**
Prep Time:	**none**
Cook Time:	**none**
On-Trail Prep Time:	**none**
Cook Time:	**5 to 10 minutes**

You can add parmesan cheese and crushed red pepper flakes if you like . Pizza restaurants usually carry small portion sized packages of each. Also, you can add any dehydrated vegetable to the pizza.

3/4 cup marinara sauce

olives, sliced

green pepper, diced

onion, diced

mushrooms, diced

1 package sliced pepperoni

2 strings of cheese

1 tortilla

1 Ziploc brand gallon-size bag

1 small freezer bag

Instructions:

At home:

1. Thinly spread marinara on parchment paper. Dehydrate at 135° F for 6-8 hours.

2. Should be a leather when dried. Tear into pieces and place into a freezer Ziploc brand bag.

3. Dehydrate olives, green peppers, onions, and mushrooms at 125-135° F for 4-8 hours.

4. Add dehydrated vegetables to the Ziploc brand bag.

5. Pack the tortilla in a gallon-size Ziploc brand bag along with 2 string cheeses and pepperoni.

On the trail:

6. Add 1/4 cup of hot water to the marinara and the vegetables.

7. Let sit 5 minutes to rehydrate.

8. Add marinara and pepperoni to tortilla. Top with peeled string cheese and enjoy.

Rick "Forrest" R. - Borden, IN, US
Ericka R. - Sellersburg, IN, US

Thru Hiker | 2015

Family-Friend

Trail Spaghetti

Tastes just like spaghetti from home!

Best for **Dinner**

Servings: **3 to 4**

Requires At-Home Prep:	**Yes**	On-Trail Prep Time:	**none**
Prep Time:	**18 to 24 hours for dehyradtion**	Cook Time:	**5 to 7 minutes**
Cook Time:	**15 minutes**		

We used rotini noodles because they are easier to eat while on the trail. You can add any dehydrated vegetable you prefer.

1 box rotini noodles

1 jar marinara sauce your preference

1 green pepper

2 to 2-2/3 cups Mountain House brand Cooked Ground Beef

3-4 each quart-sized freezer bags

salt, pepper, oregano, and parmesan to taste

Instructions:

At home:

1. Cook noodles according to package.

2. Drain and dehydrate noodles at 110° F for 8 hours.

3. Once dried, evenly separate the noodles into 3-4 quart sized freezer bags.

4. Thinly spread the marinara as evenly as you can on parchment paper. Dehydrate at 135° F for 6-8 hours.

5. Should be a leather when it is done. Split the marinara between the bags of noodles. We tore ours into smaller pieces so it re hydrates easier.

6. Dehydrate a diced green pepper at 105° F for 4-8 hours. Split between the bags of noodles.

7. Add one serving of beef to each bag of noodles (2/3 cup)

8. Add salt, pepper, and oregano to taste (We went heavy on the oregano)

On the trail:

9. Add 1-3/4 cups of boiling water to each freezer bag.

10. Let sit for 5 minutes to rehydrate.

11. Add parmesan cheese and enjoy.

Rick "Forrest" R. - Borden, IN, US
Ericka R. - Sellersburg, IN, US

Thru Hiker | 2015

Family-Friend

What's Cooking on the PCT 2016

Do you want to be part of next year's cookbook? Do you have some cool recipes and other concoctions to share with your fellow long distance hikers and backpackers? You can even submit photos – no matter if they are of food, people or scenery. Help us make this an even better book next year.

We're taking submissions now! Just visit www.cookingonthepct.com. Once there you can learn about this project – a community cookbook put together by those closest to the PCT – hikers, angels, family, friends and other supporters and followers.

This is an amazing gift to share with your friends, family, fellow hikers and all other outdoors adventurists. Based on the response of the 2015 First Edition, we aim to produce an updated book each year – one for every new PCT Class.

The most important reason we're doing this is to give back to the same trail we all fell in love with. Your donation is your recipe. Our donation is 50% of all net profits go to support the mission of the Pacific Crest Trail Association, to help protect, preserve and promote the Pacific Crest National Scenic Trail. Join the PCTA today at www.PCTA.org.

Please consider being a part of our book every year.

NOTES

Index

Made in the USA
San Bernardino, CA
01 December 2015